Photo
Puzzlemania™!

HIGHLIGHTS PRESS
Honesdale, Pennsylvania

Contents

Contents

HIDDEN PIECES

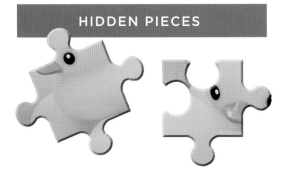

**Jigsaw puzzle challenges—
on paper!**

MATCHING

**Find the photo twins—or the
one with no match!**

GRID MAZE

**Follow the photo prompts
to solve the maze!**

SQUARE OFF

**Figure out what's in each
scrambled photo—and what
they all have in common!**

Art Class

There's more than meets the eye in this art studio. Can you find the **14 hidden objects**?

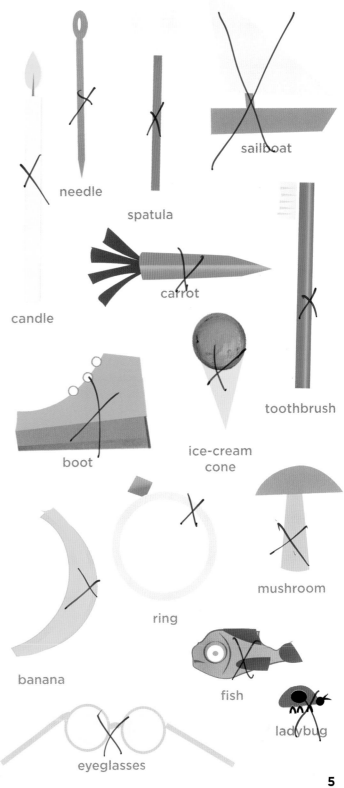

needle

spatula

sailboat

candle

carrot

toothbrush

boot

ice-cream cone

mushroom

ring

banana

fish

ladybug

eyeglasses

Catnapping

Can you find **12 differences** between these two photos?

12

Sit. Stay.

This popcorn is hiding **20 dog bones**. Can you find them all?

pone

Snack!

Under the Sea

There's a lot to see under the sea—including **16 hidden objects**. Can you find them all?

barbell

wedge of lemon

apple

sailboat

crescent moon

bird

Christmas tree

comb

glove

slice of bread

butterfly

ice-cream cone

paintbrush

flag

closed umbrella

shoe

SEE SHELLS

Each shell has an exact match.
Can you find all **12 pairs**?

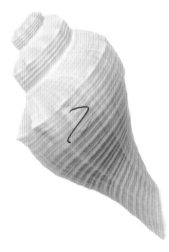

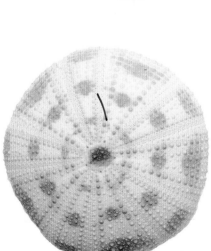

Hidden Paradise

Welcome to the jungle. Can you find the **19 hidden objects** here?

dog bone

slice of
pizza

doughnut

saw

sailboat

slice of pie

ladder

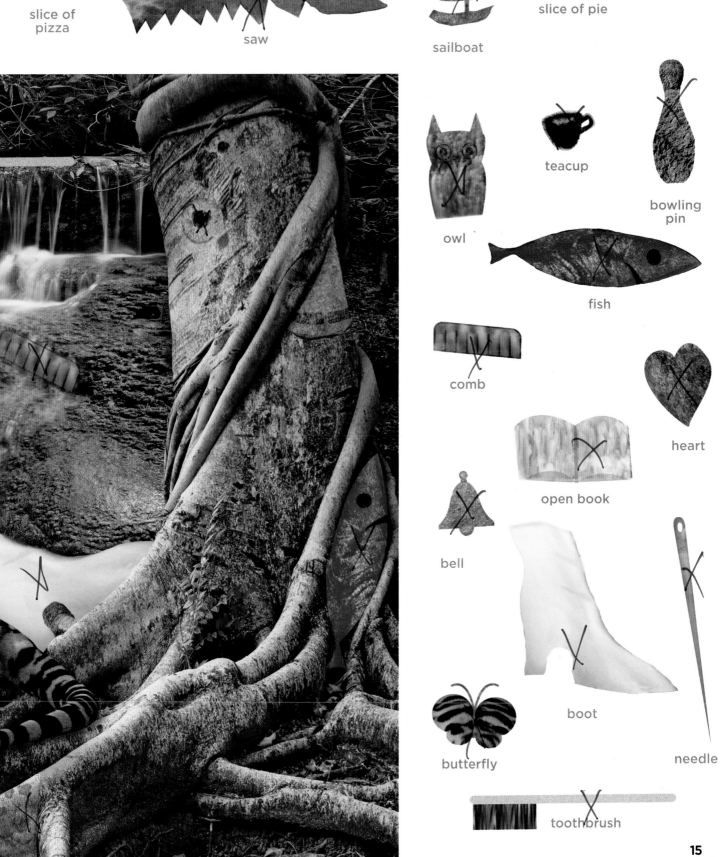

owl

teacup

bowling
pin

fish

comb

heart

open book

bell

boot

needle

butterfly

toothbrush

15

Moon Landing

Can you find **21 differences** between these two photos?

SOMETHING'S FISHY

These leaves are hiding **15 goldfish**. Can you find them all?

Look Out Below!

Jump on in and see if you can find the **20 hidden objects** in this scene.

horseshoe

mushroom

wrench

slice of pizza

kite

key

boomerang

party hat

arrowhead

needle

heart

pennant

ice-cream cone

bell

envelope

three-leaf clover

dog

golf tee

banana

necktie

Shot on Goal

Clarissa is trying to score the game-winning goal. Can you help her find the right path to the net? The symbols will tell you which way to move.

Move 1 space
RIGHT

Move 1 space

Move 1 space
DOWN

UP
Move 1 space

Move 1 space
LEFT

PATH 1	PATH 2	PATH 3	PATH 4	PATH 5	PATH 6
ball	ball	ball	ball	ball	ball
jersey	ball	ball	jersey	shin guard	ball
ball	shin guard	jersey	ball	ball	shin guard
jersey	cleat	ball	shin guard	jersey	ball
cleat	cleat	cleat	ball	shin guard	shin guard

EXIT

SEE WHAT?

Can you figure out what item appears in each picture? Once you've got them all, can you guess what they all have in common?

Earn Your Stripes

What's black and white and hidden all over? This puzzle! Can you find the **24 hidden objects**?

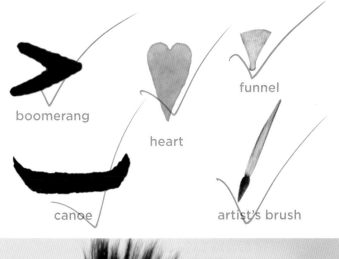

boomerang

heart

funnel

canoe

artist's brush

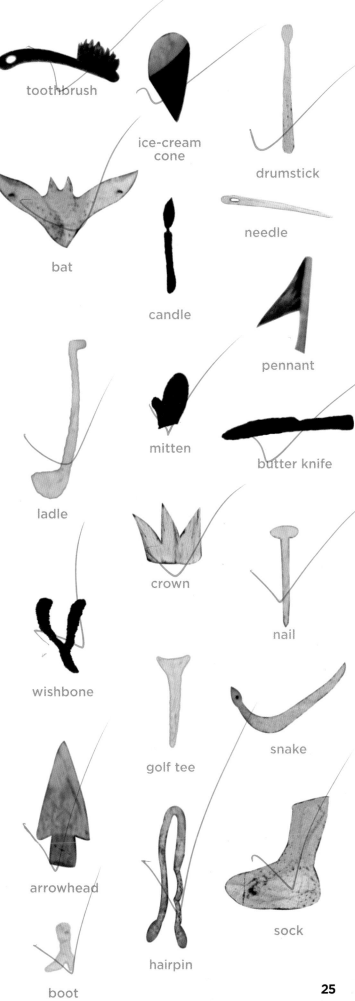

toothbrush

ice-cream cone

drumstick

bat

candle

needle

pennant

ladle

mitten

butter knife

crown

nail

wishbone

golf tee

snake

arrowhead

hairpin

sock

boot

Clowning Around

Look carefully and see if you can spot **12 hidden objects**.

cactus

basball bat

pencil

sock

flower

necklace

blueberry

necktie

bunch of balloons

marble

rocket ship

light bulb

A Pig Deal

Can you find the **one pair** of pigs that match perfectly?

CLIP IT

Can you find these **8 jigsaw pieces** in this photo of paper clips?

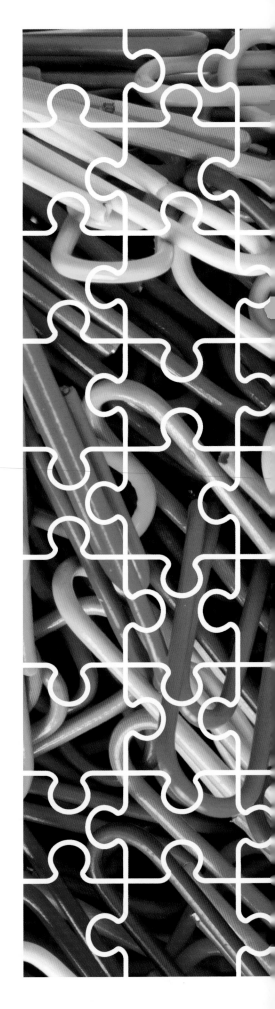

What a Ride!

Feel the fresh powder as you search for the **16 hidden objects** in this scene.

funnel

eyeglasses

shark

paper clip

baseball cap

artist's brush

candle

frog

baseball

banana

mitten

slice of pie

pine tree

spoon

slice of pizza

train

Stuffed Sofa

Can you find **15 differences** between these two photos?

COME CLOSER

Can you spot **23 caterpillars** on this leaf?

Take a Spin

Can you find **22 differences** between these two photos?

Grin and

Bear It

Can you pick out the **20 bears** hiding in this carrot crop?

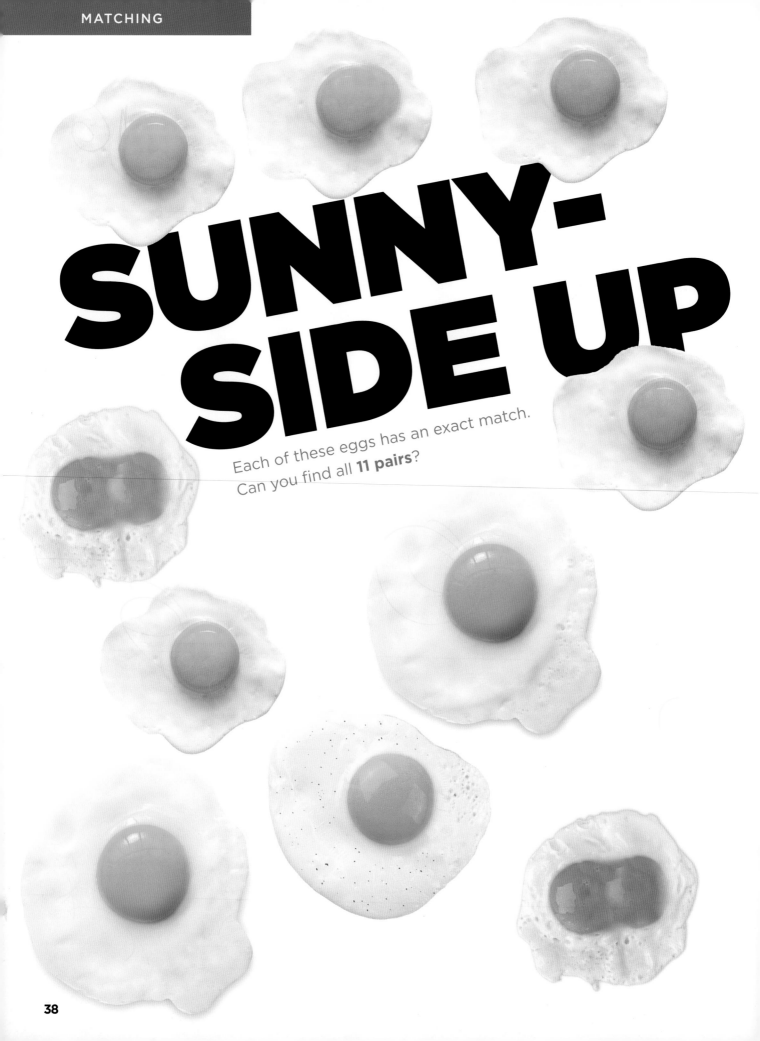

SUNNY-SIDE UP

Each of these eggs has an exact match.
Can you find all **11 pairs**?

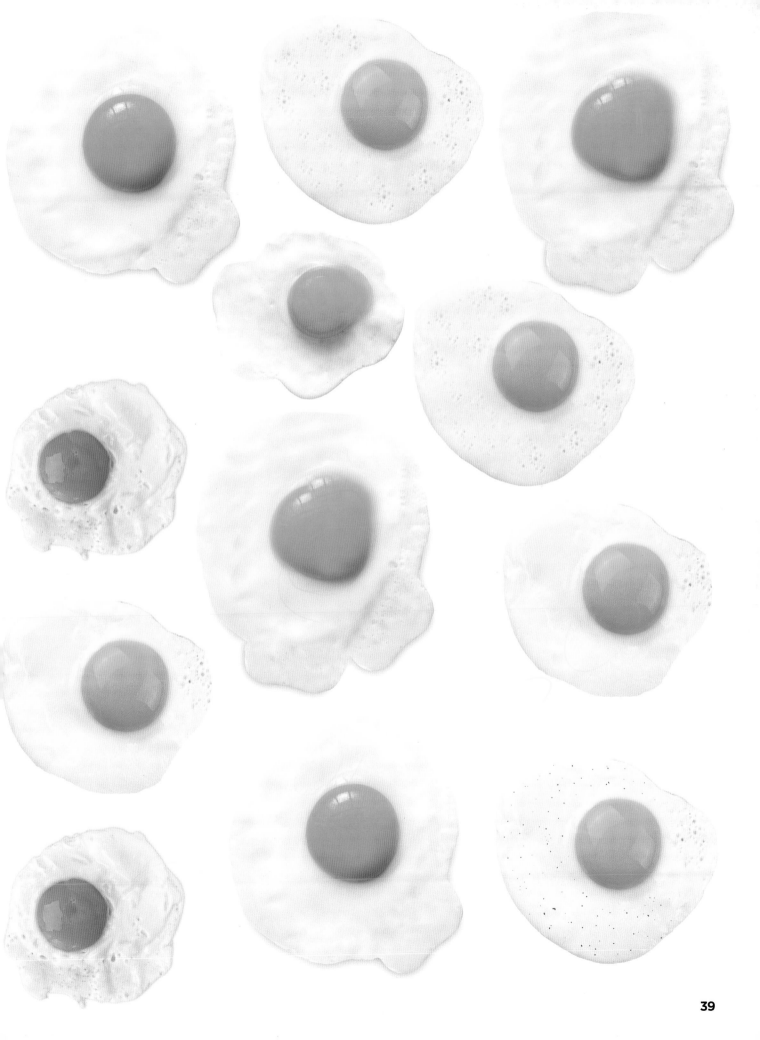

Flock Together

These birds are hiding **18 hidden objects**. Fly on in and see if you can spot them all.

shoe

dolphin

glove

mitten

heart

needle

bowling pin

teacup

toothbrush

dog

slice of cake

ice-cream cone

fish

sunglasses

rat

shovel

boot

pencil

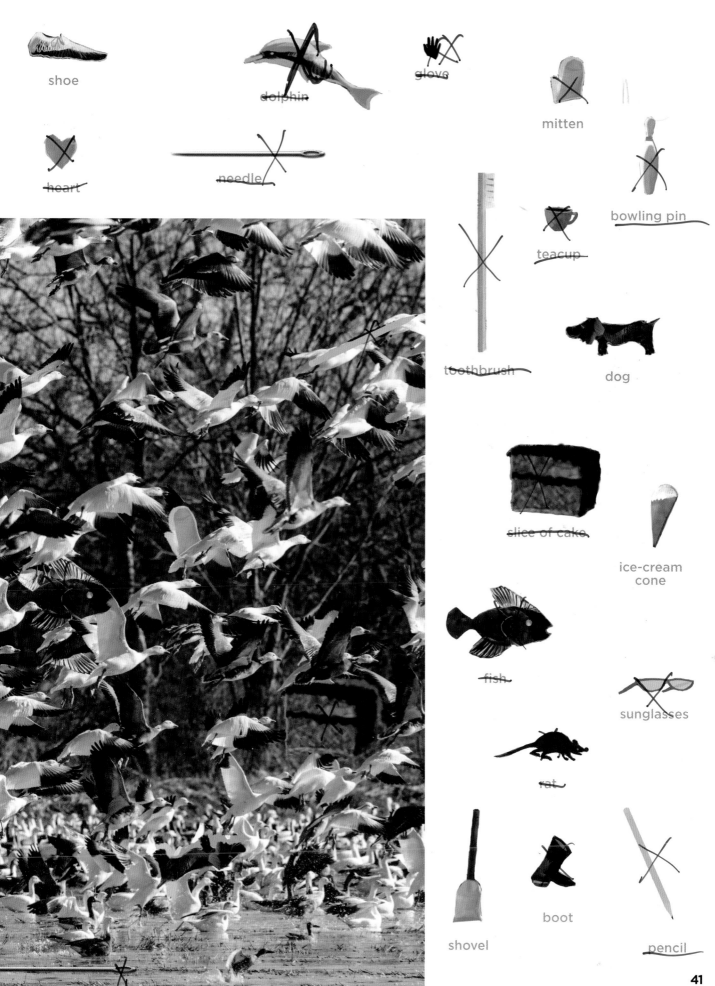

Pass the Popcorn

Can you find **18 differences** between these two photos?

I See You

Can you find all **14 hidden objects** in this photo?

dog bone

fish

key

button

lizard

kite

heart

needle

chair

slice of pie

hammer

carrot

teakettle

sock

Horsing Around

While these horses wait for their dinner, can you find the **15 hidden objects** in the barn?

needle

teacup

sailboat

heart

shovel

pencil

belt

fishhook

artist's brush

toothbrush

hockey stick

shoe

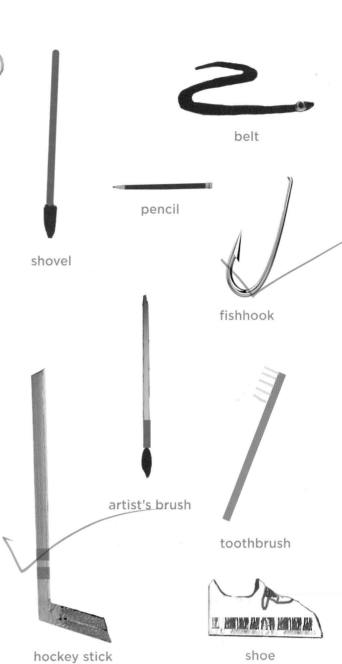

ice-cream cone

paper clip

paintbrush

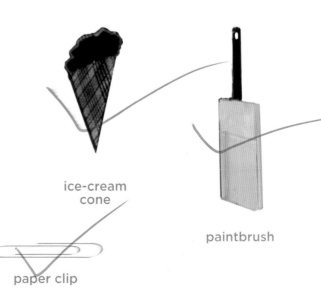

Totally Tubular

Can you find these **8 jigsaw pieces** in this photo of tubes?

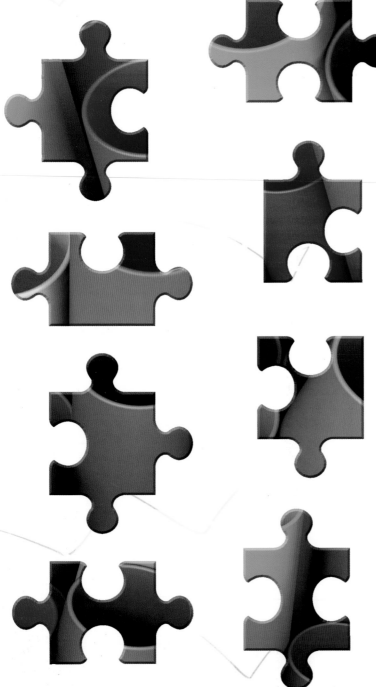

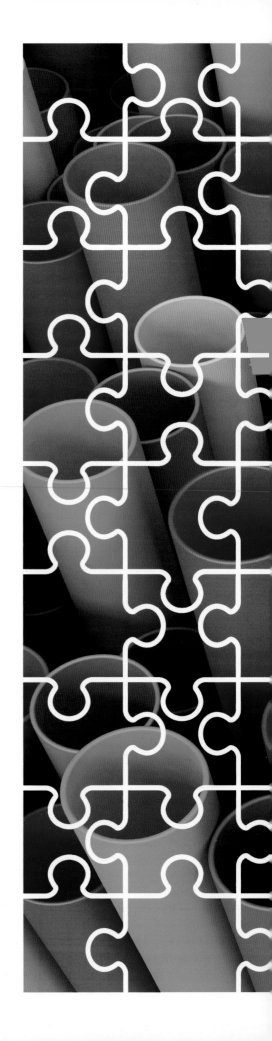

Traffic Jam

Can you find **20 differences** between these two photos?

DEEP BLUE SEA

Go fishing for the **17 hidden objects** in this scene. Can you spot them all?

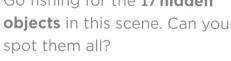

feather

pen

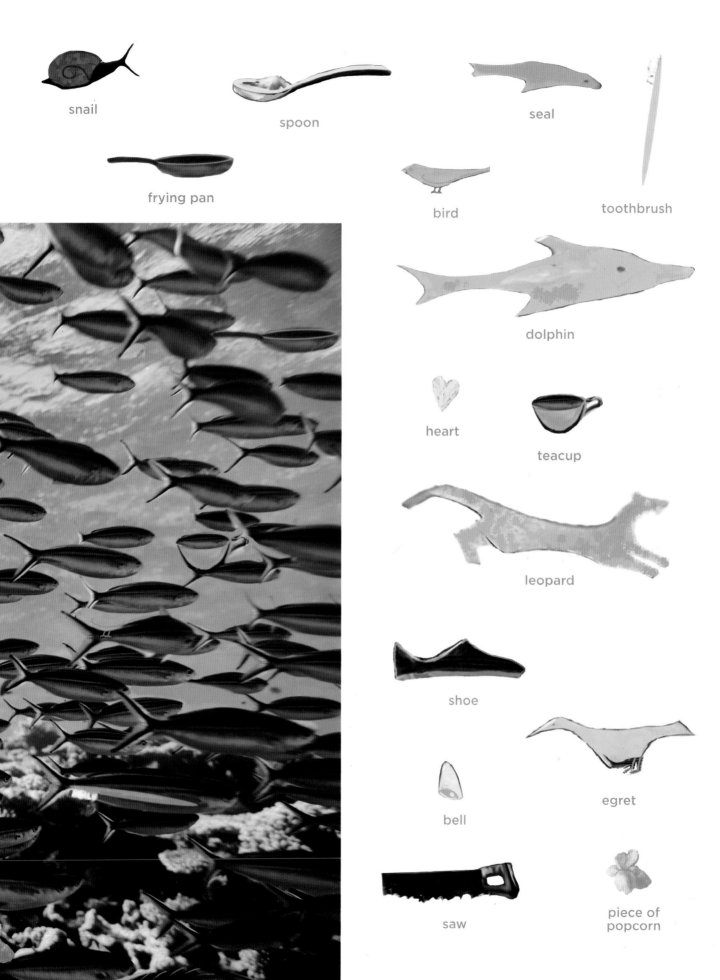

snail

spoon

seal

frying pan

bird

toothbrush

dolphin

heart

teacup

leopard

shoe

bell

egret

saw

piece of popcorn

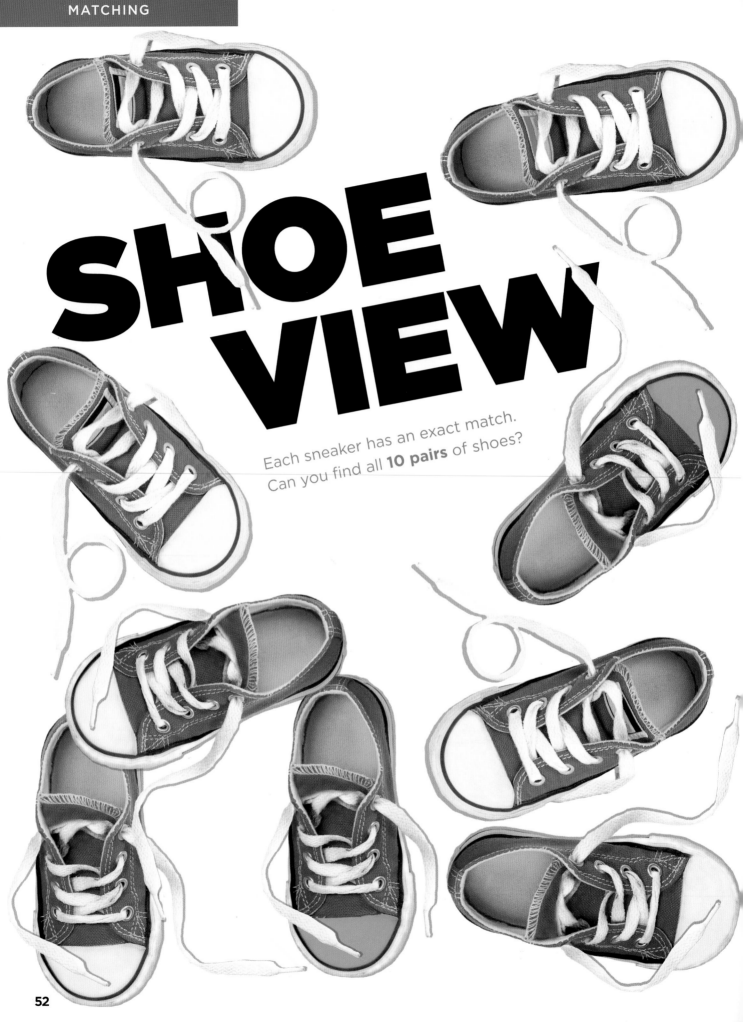

SHOE VIEW

Each sneaker has an exact match.
Can you find all **10 pairs** of shoes?

Nosy Neighbors

Can you find **21 differences** between these two photos?

Let's Go Bowling

This cereal is hiding **16 bowls**. Can you find each one?

NOT KNOTTED

Can you figure out what item appears in each picture? Once you've got them all, can you guess what they all have in common?

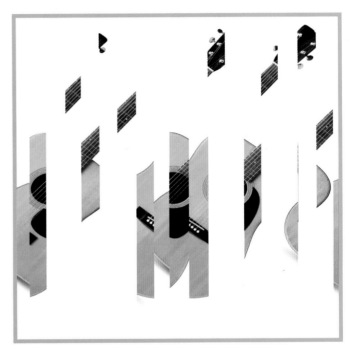

Double Chomp

Can you find **17 differences** between these two photos?

See the Light

Can you shine some light on all **12 hidden objects** in this photo?

fish

artist's brush

ice-cream cone

carrot

crescent moon

heart

mitten

shovel

sailboat

pennant

cotton candy

needle

Rock On!

There's more than meets the eye on this climb. Can you find the **19 hidden objects**?

feather

fish

slice of pizza

footprint

bird

harmonica

knitted hat

toothbrush

bowling ball

book

heart

mushroom

bowling pin

boot

handbell

sailboat

saucepan

rabbit

teacup

Penguin Poses

Can you find **21 differences** between these two photos?

SWE

There are **15 balloons** hiding among the treats. Can you find them all?

Home, Sweet Home

Bowser got lost on his way home. Can you help him find the right path to his doghouse? The symbols will tell you which way to move.

 Move 1 space **RIGHT**

UP Move 1 space

 Move 1 space

Move 1 space **DOWN**

LEFT Move 1 space

PATH 1	PATH 2	PATH 3	PATH 4	PATH 5	PATH 6
bone	bone	bone	bone	bone	bone
bone	bone	bone	ball	bone	bone
bone	collar	bone	bone	ball	bone
bone	bowl	ball	collar	bone	collar
bowl	collar	bone	ball	ball	bowl

BOWSER'S HOUSE

BUGGING OUT!

All the ladybugs but one look exactly alike. Can you find the **one unique bug**?

BUTTONED UP

These buttons are hiding
21 bowling balls.
Can you find them all?

TRACTOR

TWINS

Each tractor has an exact match. Can you find all **12 pairs**?

For the Bird

This parrot wants more than just a cracker. She wants you to find the **17 hidden objects**.

bell

mitten

heart

shoe

fish 1

glove

mushroom

fish 2

ice-cream cone

bat

slice of pie

elephant

slice of bread

sailboat

candle

needle

toothbrush

Swim Class

Can you find **14 differences** between these two photos?

This micrograph of a wood cell is hiding **26 bowling pins**.
Can you find them all?

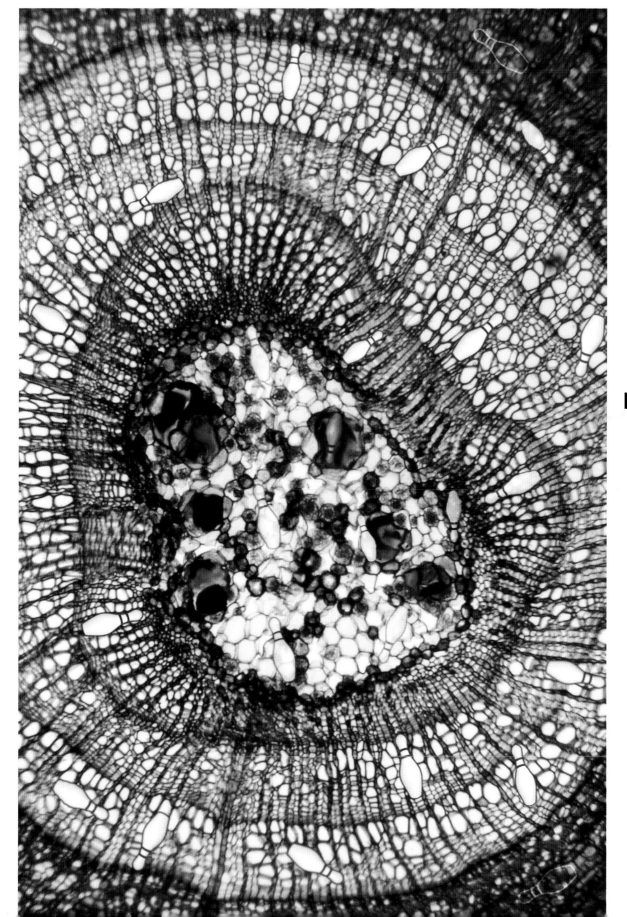

Microscopic Search

Winging It

Can you find these **8 jigsaw pieces** in this photo of butterflies?

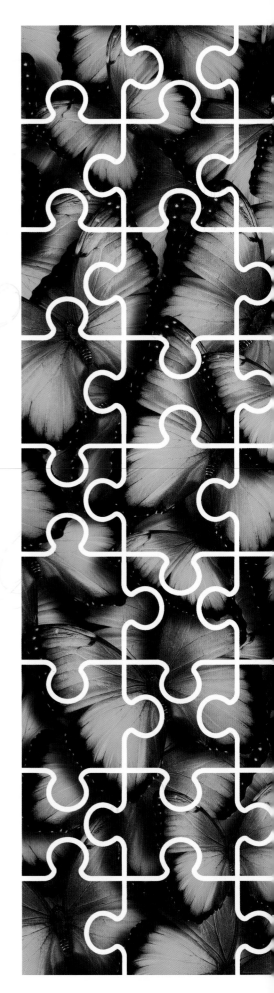

15

Hanging Around

Can you find **20 differences** between these two photos?

Heading Home

This cat doesn't seem to notice the **16 hidden objects** around her. Can you find them all?

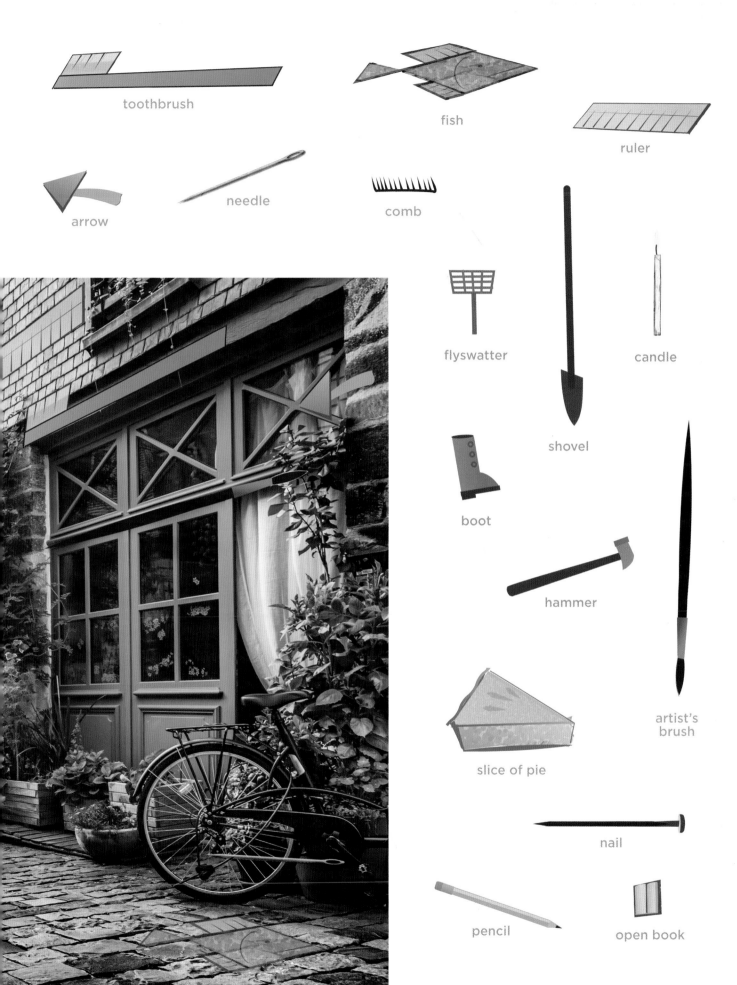

toothbrush

fish

ruler

needle

arrow

comb

flyswatter

candle

shovel

boot

hammer

artist's brush

slice of pie

nail

pencil

open book

PIGEON PAIRS

Each pigeon has an exact match. Can you find all **12 pairs** of pigeons?

LOTS OF LUCK

Can you find the **25** **horseshoes** hiding in this canyon?

Missed a Spot!

Look closely among the paint splatters and see if you can spot the **18 hidden objects**.

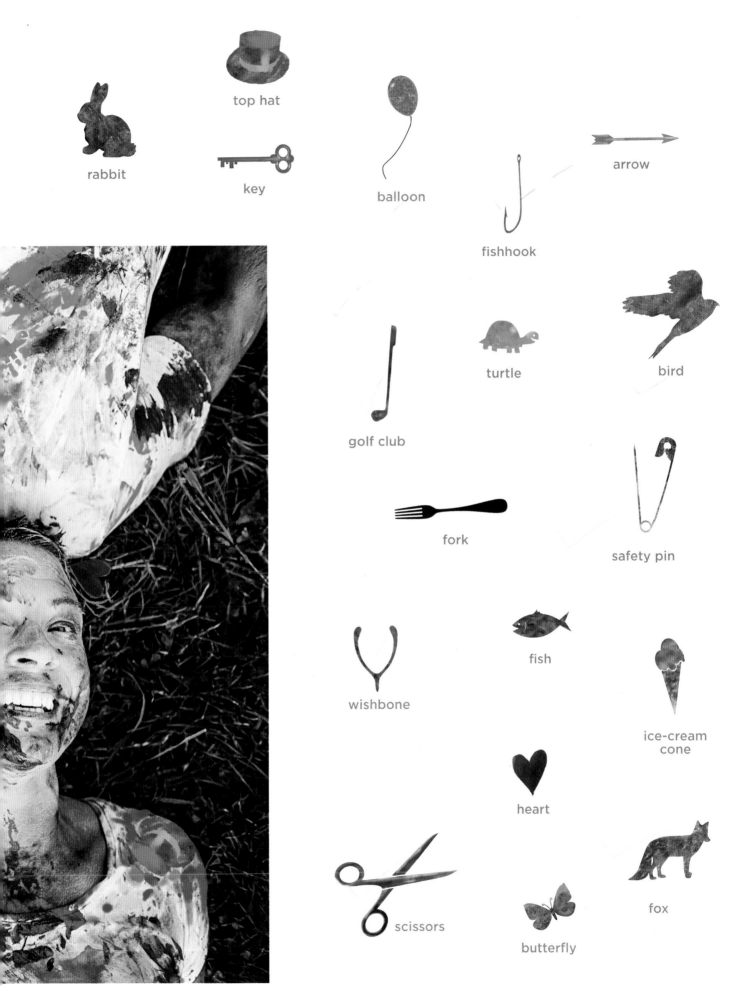

rabbit

top hat

key

balloon

arrow

fishhook

golf club

turtle

bird

fork

safety pin

wishbone

fish

ice-cream cone

heart

scissors

butterfly

fox

Moooo-ve Along

There's more in this field than cows. See if you can spot the **18 hidden objects**.

sock

necktie

mitten

crescent
moon

wishbone

artist's
brush

fish

toothbrush

chef's hat

shuttlecock

ghost

three-leaf
clover

heart

funnel

mushroom

candle

bow tie

boomerang

89

Dragon Day

Can you find **23 differences** between these two photos?

HAPPY PUZZLING!

Can you figure out what item appears in each picture? Once you've got them all, can you guess what they all have in common?

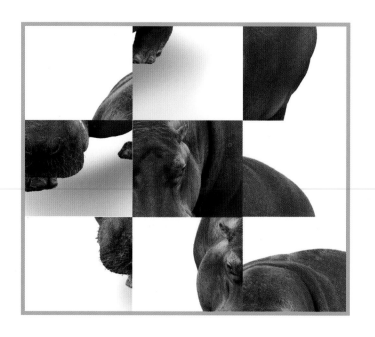

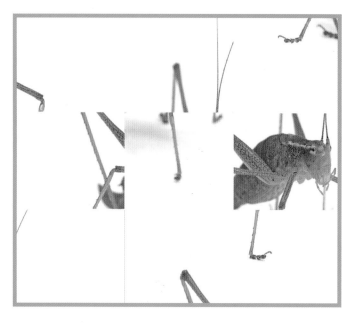

Stare Down

Can you find **12 differences** between these two photos?

Venice View

This canal in Venice, Italy, is home to cafés, boats . . . and puzzles. Can you find the **19 hidden objects**?

saw

toothbrush

spatula

slice of
pie

table

paint
bucket

drinking
straw

open
book

umbrella

golf club

candy
cane

hat

high-heeled
shoe

horseshoe

key

mushroom

lock

ruler

pencil

Just Duckies

Can you find these **8 jigsaw pieces** in this photo of rubber ducks?

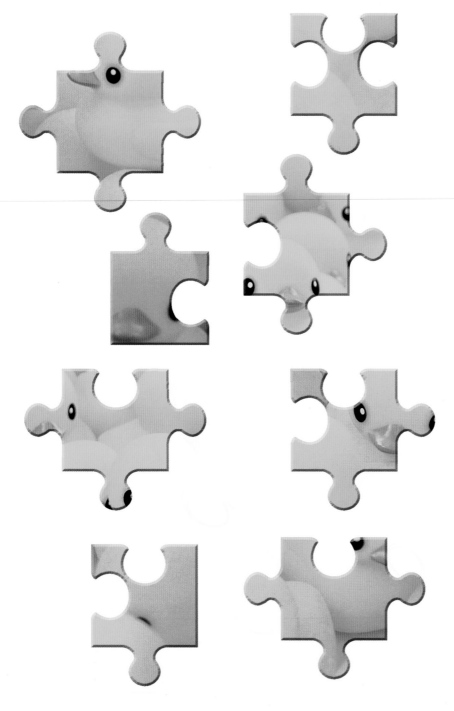

Early Bird

This bird was up so early to catch a worm that she got lost. Can you help her find the right path back to her nest? The symbols will tell you which way to move.

Move 1 space — RIGHT

Move 1 space — DOWN

UP
Move 1 space

Move 1 space — LEFT

PATH 1	PATH 2	PATH 3	PATH 4	PATH 5	PATH 6

EXIT

PICNIC POST

This picnic has more than just food. There are also **20 envelopes**.
Can you find them all? 15

Snorkel Scene

Dive in and see if you can find the **18 hidden objects** in this scene.

pencil

bell

dog bone

broccoli

ring

comb

feather

ice-cream
cone

tack

wishbone

needle

fork

glove

carrot

mushroom

banana

oven mitt

cotton
candy

WHAT'S FOR

DINNER?

Can you find **21 differences** between these two photos?

TEEING UP

There are **25 golf tees** hiding in this frigid scene. Can you find them all?

SOCK IT

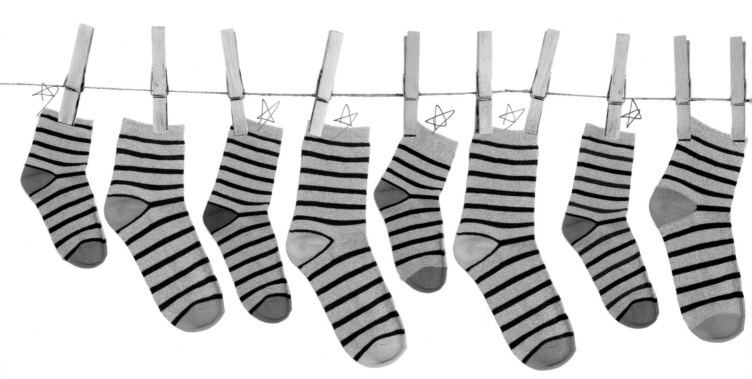

TO ME

Every sock but one has an exact match. Can you find the **one sock without a match**?

Flamingo Fun

Don't just stand around—see if you can find the **17 hidden objects** in this photo.

open book

spoon

pencil

needle

slice of pizza

heart

toothbrush

football

shoe

candle

ladder

cupcake

horseshoe

wishbone

peanut

megaphone

ice-cream cone

It's Sprinkling

There are **18 crayons** hiding among these sprinkles. Can you find them all?

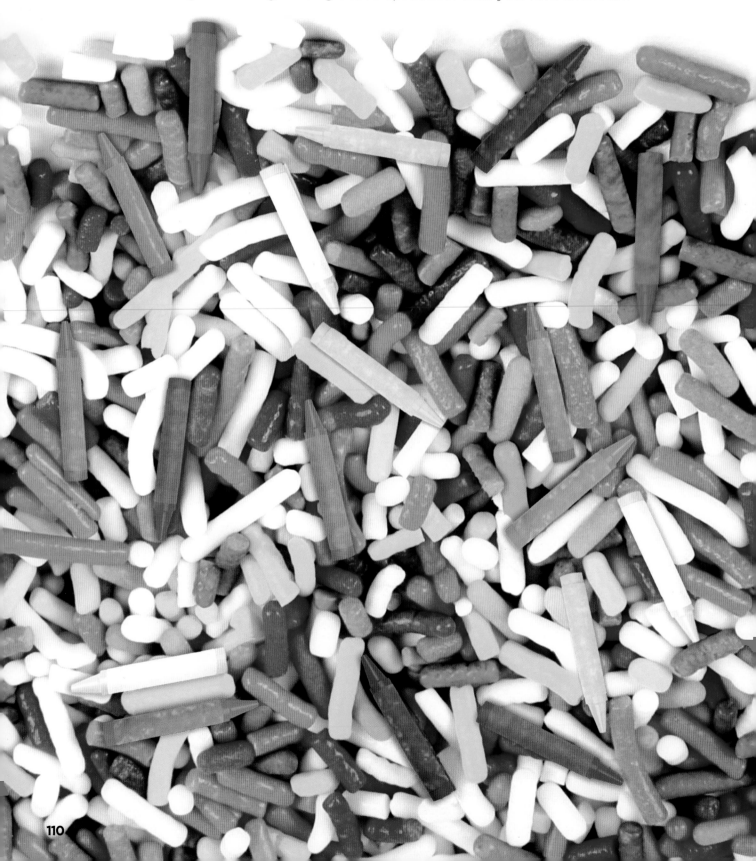

Beach Day

Can you find **20 differences** between these two photos?

Looking Up

You might need your sunglasses as you search for the **18 hidden objects** in these trees.

comb

hourglass

glove

envelope

pennant

baseball cap

fish

light bulb

ax

shovel

banana

paper clip

watering can

boot

arrow

teacup

sailboat

saw

113

FROZEN FUN

Every colorful ice pop has one that matches it exactly.
Can you find the **10 pairs**?

Hello, Ellie

This wise elephant is hiding **10 hidden objects**.
Can you find them all?

whale

feather

lizard

bird

wishbone

sock

comb

shoe

mushroom

snail

It's a Snap

Can you find these **8 jigsaw pieces** in this photo of building blocks?

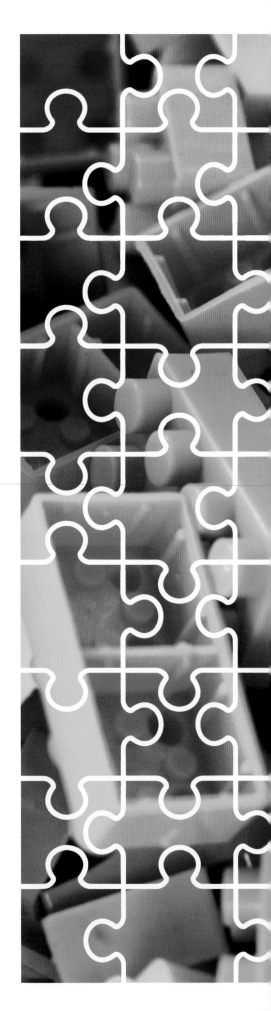

Tulip Time

Spring flowers bring . . . bananas? Can you find the **13 bananas** in this field of tulips?

Dino-Mite!

This dino is guarding **19 hidden objects**. Can you track them all down?

light bulb

ice-cream cone

heart

fish

teacup

nail

needle

slice of pizza

comb

mushroom

fish skeleton

rabbit

sailboat

bird

megaphone

feather

baseball

bell

hammer

Cookie Confusion

Each gingerbread person but one has an exact match. Can you find the **one without a match**?

122

Dresser Disaster

Can you find **21 differences** between these two photos?

BFFs (Best Furry Friends)

Sit, stay, and see if you can fetch the **14 hidden objects** in this scene.

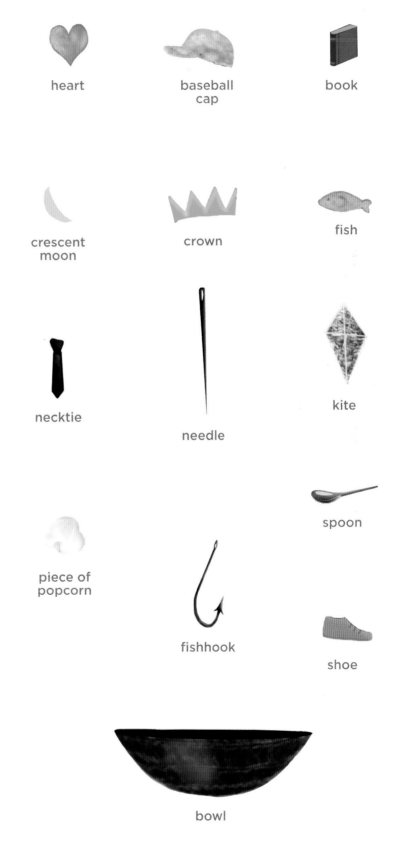

heart

baseball cap

book

crescent moon

crown

fish

necktie

needle

kite

piece of popcorn

spoon

fishhook

shoe

bowl

Going in Circles

Look around this carousel. Can you find the **18 hidden objects** riding on it?

dustpan

fried egg

slice of pizza

shoe

artist's brush

fish

slice of pie

kite

mug

domino

ice-cream cone

needle

hammer

mushroom

hot dog

train

tulip

light bulb

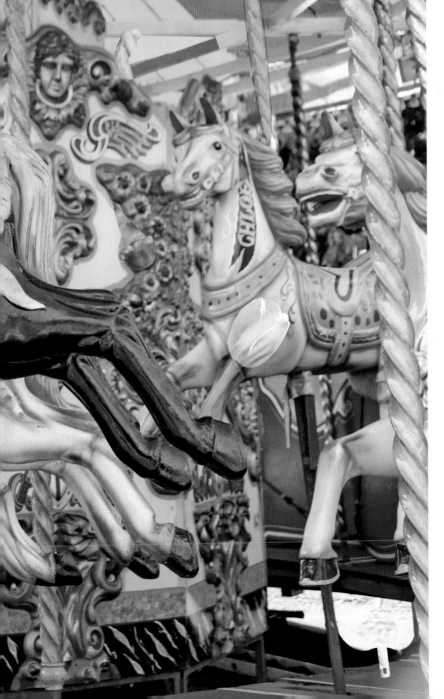

I've Got This

Can you find **15 differences** between these two photos?

▼Pages 4–5

▼Pages 6–7

▼Pages 8–9

▼Pages 10–11

▼Pages 12–13

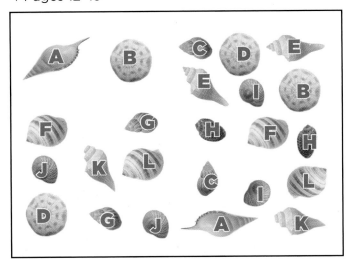

▼Pages 14–15

▼ Pages 16–17

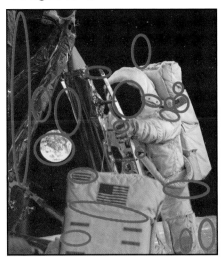

▼ Pages 18–19

▼ Pages 20–21

▼ Page 22

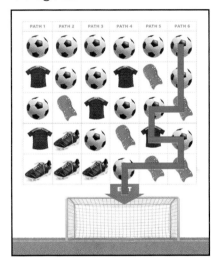

▼ Page 23

They are all animals that start with **the letter C**.

cat

cardinal

chicken

cow

▼ Pages 24–25

▼Page 26

▼Page 27

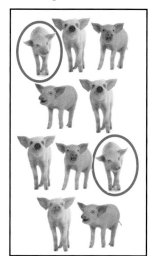

▼Pages 28–29

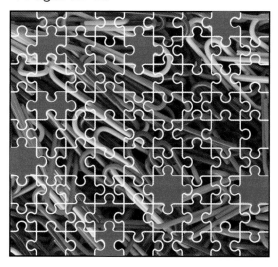

▼Pages 30–31

▼Page 32

▼Page 33

▼Pages 34–35

▼ Pages 36–37

▼ Pages 38–39

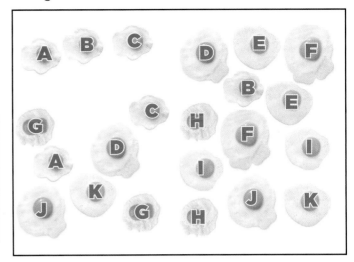

▼ Pages 40–41

▼ Page 42

▼ Page 43

▼ Pages 44–45

▼Pages 46–47

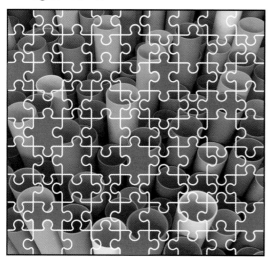

▼Pages 48–49

▼Pages 50–51

▼Pages 52–53

▼Pages 54–55

▼Page 56

They all have strings.

yo-yo

guitar

violin

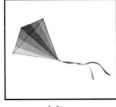

kite

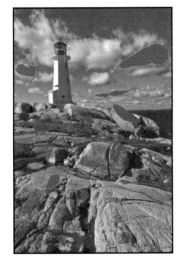

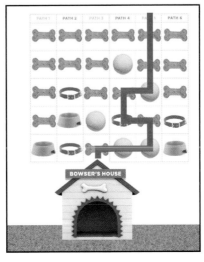

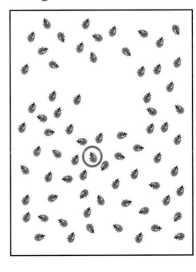

▼Pages 68-69

▼Pages 70-71

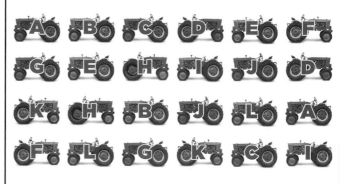

▼Pages 72-73

▼Page 74

▼Page 75

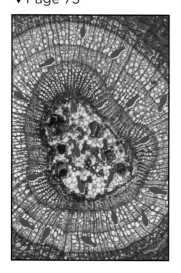

▼Pages 76-77

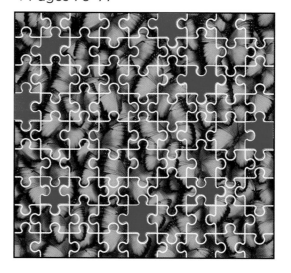

▼Pages 78–79

▼Pages 80–81

▼Pages 82–83

▼Pages 84–85

▼Pages 86–87

▼Pages 88–89

▼Pages 90–91

▼Page 92

They are all things with names that have a **double letter P**.

hippopotamus

apple

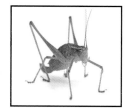

grasshopper

puppy

▼Page 93

▼Pages 94–95

▼Pages 96–97

▼Page 98

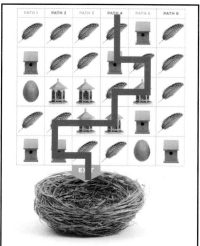

▼Page 99

▼ Pages 100–101

▼ Pages 102–103

▼ Pages 104–105

▼ Pages 106–107

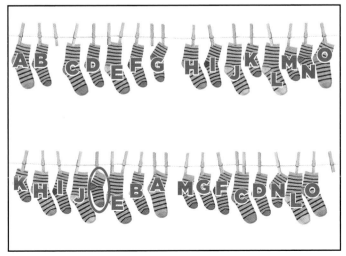

▼ Pages 108–109

▼ Page 110

▼ Page 111

▼ Pages 112–113

▼ Page 114

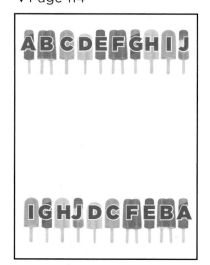

▼ Page 115

▼Pages 116–117

▼Pages 118–119

▼Pages 120–121

▼Pages 122–123

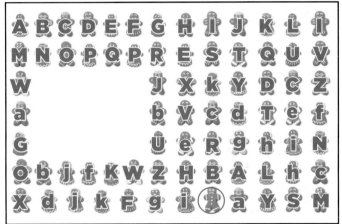

▼Pages 124–125

▼Pages 126–127

▼Pages 128–129

▼Pages 130–131

ART CREDITS

CATHERINE COPELAND (126-127); TIM DAVIS (4-5, 18-19, 40-41, 44-45, 50-51, 64-65, 72-73, 80-81); BILL GOLLIHER (8-9, 20-21, 24-25, 36-37, 56-57, 68-69, 75, 84-85, 88-89, 99, 105-106, 110-111, 118-119, 130); PETER GROSSHAUSER (26-27); KEN KRUG (10-11, 14-15, 30-31, 43, 94-95, 108-109, 112-113, 128-129); NEIL NUMBERMAN (100-101); RICH POWELL (33, 59, 60-61, 86-87, 115, 120-121)

PHOTO CREDITS

COVER: SURIYASILSAKSOM/ISTOCK (TIGER), TUNART/ISTOCK (FISH), MACIDA/ISTOCK (EGG), SWEETS-EGAL/ISTOCK (SWEETS), SMILEUS/ISTOCK (FLAMINGO), NITIMONGKOLCHAI/ISTOCK (BLOCKS), DAMEDEESO/ISTOCK (DOGS); **4-5:** SOLEG/ISTOCK; **6-7:** RASULOVS/ISTOCK; **8-9:** XXMMXX/ISTOCK; **10-11:** VITALYEDUSH/ISTOCK; **12-13:** KYOSHINO/ISTOCK; **14-15:** SURIYASILSAKSOM/ISTOCK; **16-17:** BEZOV/ISTOCK; **18-19:** RUSM/ISTOCK (LEAF BACKGROUND), IVOSAR/ISTOCK (FISH), MIKDAM/ISTOCK (FISH); **20-21:** VISUALCOMMUNICATIONS/ISTOCK (BUNGEE JUMPING), GLOBALP/ISTOCK (DOG); **22:** KARAMMIRI/ISTOCK (BLUE SHIRT), CHONESS/ISTOCK (SOCCER BALL), ROMAN SAMOKHIN/ISTOCK (SHOE), TORSAK/123RF (SHIN GUARD), SERRNOVIK/ISTOCK (GIRL), DJMILIC/ISTOCK (NET/GRASS); **23:** PAVELHLYSTOV/ISTOCK (CAT), CHAS53/ISTOCK (BIRD), SURIYASILSAKSOM/ISTOCK (CHICKEN), GERARD KOUDENBURG/ISTOCK (COW); **24-25:** JAMENPERCY/ISTOCK; **26:** TUNART/ISTOCK; **27:** BAZILFOTO/ISTOCK; **28-29:** FYLETTO/ISTOCK; **30-31:** PEEPO/ISTOCK; **32:** DORIAN2013/ISTOCK; **33:** CROSSBRAIN66/ISTOCK; **34-35:** CHICCODODIFC/ISTOCK; **36-37:** OKTAY ORTAKCIOGLU/ISTOCK (CARROTS IN GROUND), JUPITERIMAGES (TEDDY BEARS); **38-39:** MACIDA/ISTOCK, OLGAMILTSOVA/ISTOCK, EGAL/ISTOCK, MALERAPASO/ISTOCK; **40-41:** ERNIEDECKER/ISTOCK; **42:** DAMEDEESO/ISTOCK; **43:** SAG17DAS/ISTOCK; **44-45:** RTERRY126/ISTOCK; **46-47:** TOLGA TEZCAN/ISTOCK; **48-49:** SAMI SERT/ISTOCK; **50-51:** STOCK_COLORS/ISTOCK; **52-53:** ERPHOTOGRAPHER/ISTOCK; **54-55:** ADRIANDAVIES/ISTOCK; **56-57:** PAMELA_D_MCADAMS/ISTOCK, ELEMENTALIMAGING/ISTOCK (KITE); **58:** BHOFACK2/ISTOCK; **59:** LARRYHERFINDAL/ISTOCK; **60-61:** REMAINS/ISTOCK; **62-63:** MLENNY/ISTOCK; **64-65:** SWEETS-EGAL/ISTOCK; **66:** PHOTODETI/ISTOCK (DOG), MEHMETTORLAK/ISTOCK (COLLAR), JCLEGG/ISTOCK (BOWL), UROSHPETROVIC/ISTOCK (BISCUIT), CHONESS/ISTOCK (BALL), 3DMAVR/ISTOCK (DOG HOUSE); **67:** ANTAGAIN/ISTOCK; **68-69:** EGAL/ISTOCK (BUTTONS), CHEREZOFF/ISTOCK (BOWLING BALLS), TEREX/ISTOCK (BOWLING BALLS); **70-71:** RYASICK/ISTOCK; **72-73:** CAMPPHOTO/ISTOCK; **74:** DOUGHBERRY/ISTOCK; **75:** BEHOLDINGEYE/ISTOCK, RASSLAVA/ISTOCK (BOWLING PIN), GLOBALSTOCK/ISTOCK (BOWLING PIN); **76-77:** BURCHEE/ISTOCK; **78-79:** KALI9/ISTOCK; **80-81:** BLUEJAYPHOTO/ISTOCK; **82-83:** ANTAGAIN/ISTOCK, TAVIPHOTO/ISTOCK; **84-85:** CHRISBOSWELL/ISTOCK, PTASHA/ISTOCK (HORSESHOE); **86-87:** KNAPE/ISTOCK; **88-89:** TIBU/ISTOCK; **90-91:** LIUHSIHSIANG/ISTOCK; **92:** GIO_CALA/ISTOCK (HIPPO), ALEXSTAR/ISTOCK (APPLE), KNAUPE/ISTOCK (GRASSHOPPER), DOROTTYA_MATHE/ISTOCK (PUPPY); **93:** PIDJOE/ISTOCK; **94-95:** BEDO/ISTOCK; **96-97:** STEVANZZ/ISTOCK; **98:** ANDREW_HOWE/ISTOCK (BIRD), DOLE/123RF (EGG), PLAINVIEW/ISTOCK (FEATHER), GARYALVIS/ISTOCK (FEEDER), ESOLLA/ISTOCK (BIRD HOUSE), AGUADELUNA/ISTOCK (NEST); **99:** DEMAERRE/ISTOCK; **100-101:** VITALYEDUSH/ISTOCK; **102-103:** GLOBALP/ISTOCK; **104-105:** SIMONKR/ISTOCK; **106-107:** ISSAURINKO/ISTOCK (SOCKS), HANSSLEGERS/ISTOCK (CLOTHESLINE); **108-109:** SMILEUS/ISTOCK; **110:** VASKO/ISTOCK (SPRINKLES), DLERICK/ISTOCK (CRAYON); **111:** VENEMAMA/ISTOCK; **112-113:** LADY-PHOTO/ISTOCK; **114:** SUBJUG/ISTOCK; **115:** MILOSJOKIC/ISTOCK; **116-117:** NITIMONGKOLCHAI/ISTOCK; **118-119:** SUCHASJ/ISTOCK; **120-121:** SOMETHINGWAY/ISTOCK; **122-123:** THECRIMSONMONKEY/ISTOCK; **124-125:** DORIAN2013/ISTOCK; **126-127:** DAMEDEESO/ISTOCK; **128-129:** PEPLOW/ISTOCK; **130:** TADEJZUPANCIC/ISTOCK

For information about permission to reproduce selections from this book, please contact permissions@highlights.com.

Published by Highlights Press
815 Church Street
Honesdale, Pennsylvania 18431
978-1-68437-201-0 (hc)
978-1-62979-997-1 (pb)
Made in China

First edition
10 9 8 7 6 5 4 3 2

Editor: Betsy Ochester
Art Director: Marie O'Neill
Production: Colleen Pidel
Pre-Media Specialist: Tina DePew